MW00790219

The Old Testament— Simplified

Fredrick McMullen

TRILOGY CHRISTIAN PUBLISHERS

TUSTIN, CA

Trilogy Christian Publishers
A Wholly Owned Subsidiary of Trinity Broadcasting Network
2442 Michelle Drive
Tustin, CA 92780

The Old Testament—Simplified

A Beginner's Guide (From Genesis to Kings)

For information, address Trilogy Christian Publishing

Rights Department, 2442 Michelle Drive, Tustin, CA 92780.

Trilogy Christian Publishing/ TBN and colophon are trademarks of Trinity Broadcasting Network.

For information about special discounts for bulk purchases, please contact Trilogy Christian Publishing.

Manufactured in the United States of America

10 9 8 7 6 5 4 3 2 1

Library of Congress Cataloging-in-Publication Data is available.

ISBN: 978-1-68556-867-2

ISBN: 978-1-68556-868-9

Contents

Acknowledgements

Let me start with our Lord and Savior Jesus Christ with whom all things are possible.

Augustine McMullen - mom
James McMullen (deceased) - dad
Rachel McMullen - daughter (I am so proud of you)

All of my remaining family; siblings, nieces, nephews, etc.
I love every one of you.

Special thanks: to Eddie Nichols, Denise Nichols, and Chanda Donald - who's critical
reading and suggestions helped bring the manuscript to completion.

West Bemis Missionary Baptist Church - Pastor Walter Brewer

Kingdom Seekers Ministries - Apostle Larry Robinson

The Potter's House - Bishop T.D. Jakes

Trilogy Publishing Company - Tricia Horn (Account Executive) and all the dedicated staff
who assisted with this publication.

Introduction

The Old Testament - Simplified is written to give the Bible student a simple yet precise tool to empower the reader to achieve a fundamental level of understanding the Old Testament scriptures. *The Old Testament - Simplified* shows how the books from Genesis to II Kings connect together in a continuous, yet simplified manner, and that Israel is the centerpiece that bridges these books together. It is written in such a way that even a beginning Bible student can understand.

GENESIS

The Beginning

The books from Genesis to II Kings are all about God dealing with His people: Israel. God created Israel the same way He created all things; by Speaking! God speaks to a man named Abram, who is seventy-five years old, and promises him and his wife a son. The son is finally born when Abram is one hundred years old and Sarah his wife is ninety years old. Isaac grows into adulthood and later, after he takes a wife, the Bible says that Isaac begat Jacob. Jacob had twelve sons by four different women. It's through the seed of Jacob, that began with a promise to Abram, that Israel is now birthed. As you follow the story through Genesis, Israel grows into a mighty nation of people, but they end up slaves down in the land of Egypt.

EXODUS

The Departure

At this point, we find God's people are in bondage under the hand of the Egyptians, so God speaks to a man named Moses and commands him to go into Egypt and tell pharaoh to "let my people go." Pharaoh refused initially, but after a series of plagues that God wrought upon the Egyptians, Pharaoh thought it to be in his best interest to release the Israelites from their slavery in Egypt. Hence, exodus means departure or coming out; as we see God empowering Moses to lead Israel out of their bondage in Egypt. As a result, we have the Exodus or the Departure.

LEVITICUS

The Laws of God

Now that the Israelites came out of Egypt, remember, they had been down in Egypt for approximately four hundred years, so they only knew how to worship the Egyptian gods. So, God gives Moses a series of laws that the people were to follow in order to worship and serve Him properly. Hence, the book of Leviticus is recorded.

NUMBERS

The Wilderness

Once the Israelites came out of Egypt, they had to have somewhere to go. God promised them a land flowing with milk and honey called "The Promise Land." But unfortunately, the people did not believe God. Therefore, because of their unbelief, they were not allowed to go into the promise land, but God sent that generation into the wilderness. Hence, the book of Numbers gives a detailed account of Israel wandering in the wilderness for forty years as a result of their unbelief.

DEUTERONOMY

2^(nd) *Lawgiving*

At this point, the generation that came out of Egypt that had been wandering in the wilderness for forty years, except for Joshua and Caleb, have all died. Their children have been raised up, but they did not know how to worship God because they were children when Moses led them out of Egypt. Consequently, God instructs Moses to teach the law all over again to this new generation and make a new covenant with them. Moses obeys God and writes the words of the covenant in a book, and had the book placed in the side of the ark of the covenant where it could be preserved. The book would bear witness against the children of Israel after the death of Moses. Hence, Deuteronomy or the 2nd lawgiving is recorded in the Holy Scriptures.

JOSHUA

Israel Enters the Promised Land

Even though Israel has been free from bondage for forty years, yet they have not entered the promise land. Their leader (Moses) dies in the plains of Moab and the children of Israel mourn his death for thirty days. Afterward, God speaks to the war general "Joshua" and commands him to lead this people across the Jordan River and into the promise land. God let him know, "that just as I was with Moses, so will I be with thee." Therefore, Moses led the people of God out of Egypt, but Joshua led them into the promise land. Hence, God delivers on His promise.

JUDGES

The Ruling Leaders

Israel has now entered the promised land under the leadership of Joshua, but unfortunately, Joshua dies at a hundred and ten years old before all the territory is conquered. Also, the generation that went into the promise land with Joshua fell asleep and rested with their fathers. Then there arose another generation that knew not the Lord. God had warned His people not to follow after other gods and provoke Him to anger. But the people ignored the warning; therefore, God allowed the enemy to conquer His people and put them in bondage. God's people, being greatly distressed, would cry out to God, and He would raise up a "Ruling Leader" or a "Judge" to lead Israel out of bondage. This scenario is repeated time and time again throughout this book. Thus, we have the book of Judges.

RUTH

The Family

So far, these books show how God had compassion on the Israelites as a nation. The book of Ruth gives an account of God extending His compassion to one particular Israelite family who experienced difficult times or hardship "in the days that the judges ruled." This book of Ruth shows us that not only did God care about the Israelites as a nation, but He also cared about them as families. Hence, the nation of Israel, that God formed, is simply a collection of families.

I & II SAMUEL

The Transition

In the book of Judges, Israel noticed that each time that they were conquered by the enemy, all the conquering enemies had one thing in common: they all had a king. Until now, God was Israel's king. Israel now wants a king like the other nations had, so God grants their request. Hence, Samuel is raised up by God to transition Israel into a monarchy, as opposed to a people being directly governed by God himself. As a result, God gives Samuel specific instructions as to how to execute the transition. Hence, I and II Samuel are recorded.

I & II KINGS

The New Kings

After God resigned as king of Israel, Samuel follows the instructions given to him by God to execute the transitioning of Israel into a monarchy. Hence, Saul is anointed and announced by Samuel as Israel's first king. Unfortunately, Saul did not keep the commandment of God, so God instructed Samuel to reprove him and inform him that his kingdom would not continue. God then instructs Samuel to anoint David as king. Samuel obeys and David is anointed, appointed and reigns forty years until he is old and stricken in years. As David draws nigh to death, he charged Solomon his son to reign in his stead. After David dies, Solomon sits on the throne of David and his kingdom was established by God. But after Solomon's reign ended, Israel became a divided nation. The northern part of Israel retained the name Israel, while the southern part of Israel became known as Judah. Thus, the books of I and II Kings record the history of the kings of Israel and Judah.

SYNOPSIS

The Old Testament— Simplified

Acts Chapter 8, in the Bible, records that an Ethiopian eunuch was riding along in his chariot reading the book of Isaiah. A man named Philip, who was sent by God, asked, "Understandest thou what thou readest?" The Ethiopian eunuch responded, "How can I, except some man guide me?"

Printed in the USA
CPSIA information can be obtained
at www.ICGtesting.com
LVHW021636081123
762972LV00103B/3226